This coloring

Belongs to
_____

I like shiny things, but I'd marry you with paper rings.

I AM FEARLESS: RELAXING COLORING BOOK FOR THE SWIFTEST FANS

50 COLORING PAGES

+ BONUS 10 PAGES FOR NOTES & DOODLING

Dive into more of our Taylor themed books and let your love for her shine through every page!
Build the perfect collection for yourself and the best gift for the Swiftie in your life.

I AM FEARLESS: TAYLOR BOOK

A to Z illustrated book full of colorful taylor illustrations and inspirational quotes

AND FOR LANA DEL REY FANS

introducing our Lana Del Rey Coloring Book the perfect gift for the fans and lovers of lana

TAYLOR'S COUNTRY DREAMS

TAYLOR COLORING BOOK FEATURING CUTE COUNTRY GIRLS WITH INSPIRATIONAL TAYLOR QUOTES FROM HER COUNTRY MUSIC

Made in the USA
Middletown, DE
07 September 2024

60570335R00057